With Her Hair on Fire

Christy Prahl

I0518432

ROADSIDE PRESS

With Her Hair on Fire
Copyright © Christy Prahl 2025
ISBN: 979-8-9925009-7-4

Cover Art: James Griffin
Editor: Michele McDannold

Roadside Press
Colchester, Illinois

Table of Contents

"Who told you so?
That gold burns slow
like coal camper's candles all lost in the snow."

– Curtis Mathew Kirkwood (Meat Puppets,
"Up on the Sun")

The Cardinal Route

Tiny house, paint it yellow. Prune a hibiscus beside the railroad line behind the oil drums. Install a brick front porch like a Spanish colonnade. Keep bees, feed cats, build a swing set in the yard. Swing in it long after the children have left. Watch the posts unmooring from the ground as distant trains whistle out their warnings, speeding past like summer cranes heading south. Like morning, like running away.

The Raw and the Cooked

My grandfather cooking hot dogs over charcoal suddenly becomes my grandfather without a shirt, garish and immodest as he has never been, but he is a man on a muggy afternoon and these crimes are permitted. His skin sags like someone who once carried forty more pounds, like someone hoarding turnips in case the food runs out, which it did, early in life, before he moved to the dry-cleaning shop where he slept on a cot, contributing forty dollars a week to the family till.

My grandfather nearly feminine, all breasts and gut exposed to the air, though he's threatened me with a belt more than once. Just talk and military echoes, but it kept me in line, this way he showed discipline. He hands me a hot dog, plain like I like it, and starts to dress one for himself till my grandmother comes shouting from the kitchen with a shirt to put on hurry up for God's sake before the neighbors can see.

Please Try Again

If it's church I promise I had no idea. The Gordian knot of crossing the chest. Standing in line while a man in brocade put a chalk disc into my mouth. The urge to bite down. Just his two fingers and so many tongues. There had to be some purpose to it. We'd find it in the pews. This was before the Unitarian detour of 1978, where the only rule was macrame.

We returned to the capital C church when Uncle Ed died early of sepsis. The music in the hymnals refusing melody like something afraid of itself. Held deep in the throats of people who thought the Kinks might steal their children. Church is how I feel about flirting, technology, and space. Some people get it. The rest of us lie.

If I Asked You Once

What don't you understand about breaking
and entering? Be a wasp at the door left open
a crack. Sting my neck, try to hurt me, but
barge right in. Today I got stood up at the
laundromat, hauled a bindle a mile home like
a drifter kicked off a train. Now I'm drinking
a full bottle of Moscato on my own, so come
over and listen to some Loretta Lynn on this
yard-sale turntable I got for almost free.

I don't care who you are. You could be the
mailman. You could sell me a phone plan for
eighty-five dollars. Call me the wrong name.
I promise to answer.

Every One of Them, Mirrors

There was the one who called me *Hubcap* when I asked for a nickname. The one who got famous and still owes me eighty dollars. The one with a haircut like Joey Ramone, who cut me loose with a note tied to the foot of a baby rabbit. The one with a side hustle in magic, who could find the six of diamonds in your wallet.

Two years before he died – face bruised in sarcoma, his body a muslin sheet – the one who made an exception for me. The only girl he'd ever kissed, he said, and he'd do it again. You ask me why I tell you these things. It's not so much to sanctify them as to tame who I was when I loved them.

For Charlie, Who Left

Such joy, this rain. Its tiny feet. Its music of beaded curtains while it fills the feeder and finches come. Such agonized joy in its quiet reminders of dying, the soft sound that fails to drown the faulty muffler. The car goes away with its yawp to the next patch of city, but the rain stays.

We don't get this kind of steady downpour anymore. We get the rude storms, blinding red poppies on the Doppler. They chase us into basements, wreck roofs, steal tractors.

This is a rain loved by snap peas. Not dogs. One that returns my memories of all that's gone away: love and kind shoulders and a taste for strong cheese. This morning it brought back a snapshot of you playing trumpet. On a stoop. In a marching band uniform. Fingering the valves till Chet Baker came out. The air in your lungs, I thought forever.

The Plains

On the hottest night of the year, we walk
toward oxygen and toward the moon,
passing the sad campus town with just
a handful of boys coming apart in the
temperature, lingering there for summer
school with no hold on geography, catcalling
the girls, their voices half lager, half hornet.
We walk on to the farmland beyond, old
couples in clapboard who live for these
vacated summers, husbanding their horses,
so still in the field their bodies are stone.

We walk past the house with the naked man
and woman in bed playing chess, watching
through the batting of their curtains a knight
take a pawn, a mouth take a nipple, our sweat
an adhesive between us, shoulder to skin
– we'd only just met, and it hardly matters
there are eight years between us, each of

us young and alive in the dark – and we talk about music and the way you can almost see the alfalfa growing and where we plan to be in twenty years. You say anywhere with water and I think in your arms but say out loud Schenectady.

Names Among Deer

According to new research, elephants call each other by name. What about the deer?

There's a shortage of food here on the edges of town, where a child spies a buck while waiting at the bus stop. The oaks are thin, the brambleberries gone. Whitetails chew hydrangea and forget their conjugations till another spotted fawn ends up in the berm. The authorities call it thinning the herd. The deer call it colonization. They dub each other Lily Eater, Lettuce Eater, Hosta Eater, Gimpy, Milk Teat, Broken Horn, Hank.

There, two does, inseparable among the pin oaks: You're the Prettiest and No You're the Prettiest.

Second Sleep

Here I write a country song. *My baby only loves me when I wear the red wig.* It feels like a chart-topper. I should write down the lyrics but surely I'll remember *Kiss me by the sink hole* in the morning.

This is a sleep with dreams in it, with continents coming to visit. In some I am falling. In others I ride a Persian carpet over the World's Largest Longaberger Basket. In still another I am approached by a talking elk. *What say you,* wise elk? *Mind your business,* she huffs, then farts pink bubbles from her bushy tail hole.

What majesty, I think, awestruck to look inside a rogue bubble and see myself, floating through an ass-blown snow globe, a hi-fi playing Vince Guaraldi as I drift.

Ekphrastica
On the paintings of Dory Whynot

A girl with her hair on fire is every girl. Bring her flowers and watch her wick them to kindling. You are a fool to think nasturtium ever solved for overheating. Bring her antlers instead. Bring her your exposed clavicle. Bring her three doors to choose from. Hide a horse behind one. Your darkest secret behind another. Something to hurt behind the last. Hope she chooses Door #3. You know her only medicine is to punch from the shoulder, and she would never do that to a horse.

Where Nothing Misbehaves

Streets are named for presidents or trees, each house a declaration: *these pillars could be yours.* Anchor of a red front door, clean verticality of painted shutters. Pets asleep in identical curl, tiger cat in a window frame, yellow lab on a braided rug. Mailboxes closed for road appeal. Neighbors spray the dandelions dead, mow their lawns like crewcuts.

Admit it. You can see yourself here.

The widow farmer refuses to sell, her land rich with mineral, a dozen sheep grazing clover in a field. She is the wife of a dead veteran and no one will make a memorial of her. Today's listings include floor plans and directions to turn right at the red barn and follow the curving road, all the way in, away from the city and everything else.

An Introvert Prepares to Reenter the World

I've spent the last hour testing my legs to see
if I can move them. Two steps past the bed,
one more past the mailbox. The bedsheets
say no. The soft curl of dog says no. The
hectoring sun says maybe. Is someone out
there waiting for me? Do you hear my name
through fields of razor-wheat in your sleep?
Do you mind if I collapse into the cup of your
arms?

I've put myself here in a room without
windows, walled against the keratin inside
the word *there*. Only fools heave up on its
syllable. A single phoneme in the likeness
of a hoof, severed and left in the woods
for gleaners to wonder *what in the world?*
The hunter knows. In the sight of his rifle
the promise of antlers for the wall. Meat for
months, ripe for a slather of huckleberries.

Orange vest to distract from the terrible, genital configuration of his face. He may see you and shoot.

Don't look at him, I tell myself. Don't imagine him in a deer blind, mistaking you for a stag. Just notice the brave movement of your shoes.

An Apology for Trivial Living

Let's be honest about the hustle. I've become neither modern dancer nor pastry chef. Neither engineer nor biographer. My shortfalls could bankrupt the lead of a pencil.[i] We are, as humans, a dissertation in the mundane. There may be three or four greats who occupied busses or punched hearts back to beating and measurably changed the arc of this sick world. For the rest, the details of our waking hours tax the patience of strangers. Trailing off to think of that dripping faucet that needs fixing or the neighbor they imagine kissing in subterfuge behind the garage. You're doing it now.[ii] Our dead parents have little to crow about in their infinitely boring afterlives cleaning litter from the side of celestial roads. I keep a full lunar eclipse in my desk to remind myself it's still possible to be stunned by the weather.

i The inventor of the attached eraser was denied a patent and lost every dime.

ii Red velvet cake is delicious.

Genteel

I imagine a courteous thief. Unarmed, disarming, patient at the garage door as I ready my bike for an eight-mile commute. *I will be taking this* / he says, peeling the handlebars from my fingers as a robin carries bits of newspaper to the gutter overhead. I release my grip faithfully, like some elegant logic commanded it. There is no axis more central to this rotational pull / and off he goes, feet to my pedals, bum to my leather seat, legs swung wide in victory as he tips his straw bowler in my direction. There I am, bikeless and bewildered, confounded how to get to work / mulling the subway or just not showing up at all. Contemplating my own pretty crimes.

Immaculate

Scouring is not for the weak when it comes
to the remains of a roast. Some call this a
chore and others the fine art of cleanliness.
If you're lucky, this second group will invite
you to dinner, and you can be sure the
napkins are laundered and no tasted spoon
has reentered the soup.

They say the more brutal the hands, the
tidier the house. My hands are red with
tributary, my house ready for you, anytime.
Come sleep in the folds of its sheets. Hide a
note beneath the pillow. Know it will leave a
slice in my thumb, so make it say something
nice, like I love you.

Stripping the Beds

The visitors have left. Muted hum where showers were running. Chirps of morning radio, still. Ripe apples left in a bowl.

A woman calms at the sight of a robin, flying to the gutter for yesterday's rain. Her guests have gone their clumsy ways, coffee cups and soda cans left behind chairs, damp towels on hooks awaiting the hamper. The floors need sweeping, the sink a good scrub. But here, an empty chair for reading. For refusing.

Hummingbirds

They arrive each summer and multiply, drawn by nectar in a red plastic feeder. Skilled conductors we are, obliging nature to behave, courting the industrious straws of their beaks.

They hover vertically before the attack. A dominant green bunts a red-throated black for hoarding too much sugar, a brutality inconceivable in something so small.

In better weather, we watch as they dance. If we are dusting the house, we go still to prolong it. If arguing, we pause to their audible whir. Such power, we think smugly to ourselves, the ways we can bend it.

Backcountry

Today the sun comes up east while the moon
loiters west, scolding and whole, and we are
swallowed in the same argument from last
week like a shirt we've worn camping, ripe
with our negligence, ignoring it away but
never quite buried, stuffed in the corner till
we open the rainfly to let in the air but what
enters instead is that moody expression,
all craters, sure, but we see a mouth and
slingshot to the chiseled lines of our own
antipathy, solid as limestone, talking always
slipping into shouting, our tools dull our
desire duller, yielding to this cadence as
predictably as sun to moon to moon to sun
holding up opposite sides of the sky.

Night Vision

No one loves the ballad of a woman losing her looks. Drench her in the dark morning when she wakes from the need to piss, her body withering to the indignities of age, slouched like the sad tree outside the window, the one that should be stump-ground but still produces apples.

Face sagging and ink-lined, flimsy as a grocery bag, mouth flattened to a scowl over all that has disappointed her in this once hopeful life. Poor sleep. Demanding children. She once saw a satellite flickering above, collecting its intelligence. She imagined it falling in love with her. The episodes in her gait, the silver reflecting from the top of her head.

Alentejo

I've gone just down the street and all the way to Portugal to run away from my life. Found asylum on a sprawling farm where skirts of cork get peeled from trees to stop up the grenache. I can pick a lemon from a branch outside my door. I can forgive our very last argument for nearly doing us in.

I borrow this life and its pillowcases swaying gently on the line and contemplate thread counts and other mathematics. Chickens wake me in the morning before their throats are slit for dinner. The hours consume me slowly, with intention. Later, the sun will set over the vineyards. Broad beans will snake around fencing, disguised as ardor. We are together in history but held apart by this map, red lines crossing over blue, each turn a steady reminder of how far we've come and gone.

Everything Plugs into Everything Else

The rechargeable battery into the laptop into the wall. The holiday lights into the next row of holiday lights into the extension cord into the floor. The clock into the power strip with the glowering red button. A hostile constancy but one that says the mechanics of everyday life are humming. We copper the strands and believe in those strands, which keeps them conducting. No old house was built for the grid, yet its outlets are all that contain me.

I overload its circuits as I hike the furnace that forces warm air through the duct work and into my bitter feet. I plug into this sweater into these sleeves into the morning light. I'd put my finger in a socket but know it would send a jolt through the system, this bungalow finally taxed of its patience. Instead I plug a finger into myself and realize it's not hard to invent electricity.

Please Send Regrets

I ask my neighbor to join me for dinner before I realize I'm over my skis, not wanting to leave the house after all. It sounded so bright for a minute, to go where other people go, to eat the chicken with a knife and fork delivered in an origami napkin. Unravel it like a straitjacket, I would. Eat with the fork in the proper hand. Keep up conversation as if the world is not laden with yellow jackets.

My husband nearly died of anaphylactic shock but a pen with a needle saved his life. Is this the kind of thing one discusses at dinner? It sounded so humane, there under the lights with people who ask you kind questions. I am not fit for this world sometimes. Other times, sure, buff me in, but today I arched out my foot and came back without a shoe.

Be-Spoke

What language is this, when a whippet is both a dog and a drug? Darn a cry of frustration or what the thrifty do to a sock. A spoon a tool for oatmeal or cradle for the body we love. A donut to assault the teeth or cushion our private sores.

In the end do we want the whole or the hole, I ask without entendre. It's so elegant to pare a pear, three times as we repair it all, when all is both a universe and stabbing tool. Good mourning, my dove, your sweet minor coo. But now we've slid into our homophones, where their is they're is over there, and here is where we listen.

The Return

Ease gently into a woven chair, unsteady after years of standing (by which we mean the body or the chair?) Sit, but sit softly, without a plate of food in the lap. It's June and our love is archival, trimmed as a beard. Long days, blank as winter, both of us too tired to carry a grudge. A friend's child sees some giddyup in our eyes and suddenly we are adoring. We pretend to crack an egg on her head, membrane oozing down the side of her face as she laughs and nearly believes it.

Who are we but these simulated eggs, intact until we aren't. It takes so little to break us apart, yolks unglued and combed through the whites. Fragile but vital ingredients. Sprinkle the shells on the garden to make the radishes grow. Some fecundity left in us after all.

Sift

We return from a week in Port St. Lucie, heavy with conch, to the evidence of squatters. Tributaries of cracker crumbs. Punctured boxes of dry rigatoni. Scat.

We're descendants of the Depression and despise this waste, despise even more the perforation of this house. We'll decode it on knees that argue with us, folding into the cliches of man and woman with an ease that later embarrasses us. He investigating the perimeter for cavities, shoving steel wool into cracks in the foundation. Me assessing what can be saved. Peanut butter skimmed of its upper layer. Cans of navy beans, unmolested. A single sleeve of butter cookies. The rice and walnuts need to go.

We're quietly shamed by this deficit, losing a

gamble to mice, but we'll eat dinner tonight
ignoring what their tails have touched, proud
of all we've salvaged.

Soon, the Crocus

Fear is what keeps us from stupidity, says the
therapist. I am much less stupid and afraid
these days. My love is an audience. I will
reach for his leg and test my bravado. He may
refuse me, shifting my arm to his waist as he
begs five more minutes / a parachute in his
voice.

And so we wake together to these new
lives, blankets mussed, birds too loud for
morning courtesy. We angle toward the sun
knowing there is not one hour taken up with
obligation. Our pallets are empty and stacked
in the garage. We begin with our walls / safe
from animals. We are primates with egos.

We may use them later to build a crossword
or a chicken stew. Joint projects that put the
we back in weld, west, and sweater. A thing to
fuse, a place to visit, a way to stay warm. He
keeps my arm around him like a belt /
a beginning.

Acknowledgements

Many of these poems found their first home in journals, and I'm grateful to acknowledge the following editors and curators who believed in my work.

"Alentejo," *Eastern Iowa Review*
"An Apology for Trivial Living," "Ekphrastica," "Genteel," and "Please Try Again," *Public School Poetry*
"Every One of Them, Mirrors," *SWWIM*
"Everything Plugs into Everything Else," and "The Raw and the Cooked," *Glint*
"If I Asked You Once," "Immaculate," "Names Among Deer," "Sift," "Stripping the Beds," "The Cardinal Route," and "Where Nothing Misbehaves," *Eunoia Review*
"Night Vision," *Lindenwood Review*

My deep appreciation for the eyes and ears that landed on these poems in their infancy, especially Robert MacDonald, the PenRF community, and the City Lit Bookstore monthly poetry salon.

To my Dairy Hollow witch pod – especially Leslie Von Holten, who keeps a refuge for my soul in Kansas – thank you for the support to keep me going.

To Michele McDannold of Roadside Press, your care for small press publishing and your ragtag crew of authors is dedication nonpareil. I'm so grateful this collection found a compass to you.

And to John, my book light, occasional sparring partner, and dearest familiar for over half our lives, my corner is incomplete and unspeakably boring without you. Eternal thanks for cushioning it.

Christy Prahl (she/her) is an Illinois Arts Council grant recipient and the author of the poetry collections *We Are Reckless* (Cornerstone Press, 2023) and *Catalog of Labors* (Unsolicited Press, forthcoming 2026). A Best of the Net and three-time Pushcart Prize nominee, her work has been featured in *Poetry Daily* as well as many national and international journals, including the *Asheville Poetry Review, CALYX, Louisville Review, Sugar House Review, Salt Hill Journal, Penn Review, Tar River Poetry,* and others. She splits her time between a small workers' cottage in Chicago and refurbished Quonset hut in rural southwest Michigan. More at https://christyprahl.wixsite.com/christy-prahl.

"There's a lovely meander to Christy Prahl's prose poems, a precision, a grace, a natural drift that follows the path a mind wanders through memory, emotion, and sensation. They move freely in multiple directions, from wry to tender to surreal, pinning down small moments like butterflies to a spreading board. I could read a thousand pages of them." – Justin Hamm, author of *O Death* and *Drinking Guinness With the Dead*

"Annie Ernaux just won the Nobel Prize for writing great things in miniature. Christy Prahl writes even tinier pieces and with as much talent and intensity. In *With Her Hair on Fire,* she lights up the page with words that punch like poetry and tell stories like prose. There are so many interesting narrators / speakers in this collection, and I trust them all. Everyone knows their own joy and hurt. It's a pleasure to hear their words. In one amazing poem, she writes, "It's not so much to sanctify them as to tame who I was when I loved them." These poems sanctify us all. An entire universe of people trying to find a way to love and work and survive happens on these pages. There are railroads. There are hotdogs. Punkers show up to hear Joey Ramone. Hummingbirds show up at the feeder, ready to fight for sugar. The chickens will wake you up before they become dinner. I hear Denis

Johnson in these pieces. I hear Jean Rhys. I hear the magnitude of Prahl's imagination. I feel like I could quote every piece in this collection. In one poem, Prahl writes, "The Kinks might steal our children." Rock n' roll always does that. So does Christy Prahl. Open this book and you'll stop the world to finish it." – Dave Newman, author of *Better than The Best American Poetry*

"Prahl's collection bursts with melodious brevity, packing a punch. Each piece is stunningly wrapped and delivered to the reader page after page as a glimpse into a sacred time and place. *With Her Hair on Fire,* is powerful, yet subtle, unforgettable. Read it! You'll be happy you did." – Jennifer Juneau, author of *Maze*

"With poems that shimmer like roadside heat, *With Her Hair on Fire* maps the liminal spaces between domestic ritual and personal rebellion, where solitude is sensual and mid-life love is the belt of a cinched-tight arm. The mechanics of these poems are humming. Christy Prahl understands the absurd majesty of primates with eggs in a world where no one quite connects the way they should and yet – everything plugs into everything else." – Amy Baskin, author of *Skull* and *Night Hag*

MORE ROADSIDE PRESS TITLES

MORE ROADSIDE PRESS TITLES

MORE ROADSIDE PRESS TITLES

www.ingramcontent.com/pod-product-compliance
Lightning Source LLC
Chambersburg PA
CBHW031239120626
46545CB00003B/1191